The Second Book Of

# Wit & Wisdom

Basil Jackson

Scholars' Press
Oxford Graduate School
Dayton Tenn 37321

Note for Librarians: A cataloguing record for this book is available from Library and Archives Canada at www.collectionscanada.ca/amicus/index-e.html
ISBN 1-4120-9169-1

*Printed in Victoria, BC, Canada. Printed on paper with minimum 30% recycled fibre.*
*Trafford's print shop runs on "green energy" from solar, wind and other environmentally-friendly power sources.*

Scholars' Press
Oxford Graduate School
Dayton Tenn 37321

and

*Offices in Canada, USA, Ireland and UK*

**Book sales for North America and international:**
Trafford Publishing, 6E–2333 Government St.,
Victoria, BC V8T 4P4 CANADA
phone 250 383 6864 (toll-free 1 888 232 4444)
fax 250 383 6804; email to orders@trafford.com
**Book sales in Europe:**
Trafford Publishing (UK) Limited, 9 Park End Street, 2nd Floor
Oxford, UK OX1 1HH UNITED KINGDOM
phone 44 (0)1865 722 113 (local rate 0845 230 9601)
facsimile 44 (0)1865 722 868; info.uk@trafford.com
**Order online at:**
trafford.com/06-0923

10 9 8 7 6 5

2

# Preface

One might well wonder what a surgeon, psychiatrist, theologian, and lawyer would have to say in the nature of writing some wit and wisdom, particularly if one were to confine the meaning of the word, "wit," to describe something as humorous. After all, surgery, psychiatry, theology, and law all deal with conflict.

Well, sort of. In surgery, there is a biological, medical conflict between how the body functions "normally" and some biological abnormality that prevents a normal healthy function. In psychiatry, the conflict may be biological, chemical, or mental where the conflict is between healthy mental and psychological well-being, and some biological, chemical, or mental factor that prevents one from functioning appropriately. In theology, the conflicts are much more serious because they represent the gulf between how God created and intended His human creation to be, and how that was spoiled by sin. At a fundamental level, is the conflict between human kind and God because of the consequences of sin. And, for the lawyer, well, if God created the universe out of chaos, the question may be asked, who created the chaos?

But, there is more than the simple idea of humor in the word, "wit." In addition to representing the talent for speaking or writing amusingly, aptly, cleverly, and unexpectedly, with the juxtaposition of ideas and expressions calculated to delight an audience, it also describes the faculty of thinking and reasoning, of understanding, and mental cleverness, good sense or judgment, in which part of wisdom is represented in prudence and discretion. Wisdom represents the combination of experience and knowledge, with the ability to apply them judiciously, expressing the essence or nature of God, and of His will through wise sayings or precepts.

All of which is to say, these ideas all describe the talents and gifts possessed by Dr. Basil Jackson, a surgeon, psychiatrist, theologian, and lawyer. Thus, this Second Book of Wit & Wisdom, is more than a collection of quotable proverbs. It will both delight the reader, and provoke thinking and reasoning, leading the reader to better understand the essence and nature of God, and to act with judgment and prudence so as not to bring shame and reproach to His name.

Rollin Van Broekhoven
Federal Judge
Washington, DC

### The Rear View Mirror

I was born in the County Tyrone, Ireland, near the little town of Omagh, on the afternoon of Sunday, June 19th, 1932 and perhaps to be born on a religious day of rest was a prognostic sign for the rest of my life. My parents were simple, honest, hardworking and very devout. Neither of them had gone past the third grade and yet for them "education" was presented as the great hope for their four children.

I was the fourth and last child and was probably a "mistake". The psychological ramifications of this thought were clarified only thirty years later within the experience of prolonged psychoanalytic training. Whatever the reason, I became addicted to "knowing" and the search for knowledge became the prime motivating force of a life filled with an insatiable curiosity about people and reality. I still remember as a child saying to myself, "I want to know everything before I die." Some wishes are never granted!

Two of my early recollections are of interest in this regard. Both, as far as I can reconstruct the past, occurred during my fifth year.

Firstly, I remember, on a summer day, lying on my back out-side our cottage and contemplating "the wild blue yonder." I kept trying to understand if the sky had an end and if so what would be beyond that point. Perhaps that was the genesis of my life-long pleasure of being a pilot! At that time I had no awareness whatsoever that I was trying to conceive of space and infinity, but I do recall very clearly that as I struggled with these notions I began to develop a headache. In at least a metaphorical way that headache has remained with me most of my life. I also find it fascinating that later in life I came to the conclusion that a useful way to understand the concept of God is the reification of space.

The second recollection is still confusing to me after all these years. I recall exactly where I was standing when the event occurred. My sister, who was about five years my senior, was apparently trying to correct my English grammar. The statement I was making referred to my physical location on Sundays and I stated, "I be in Sunday School on Sundays." My sister tried to convince me that I should be saying that I am in Sunday school on that day. However, I was just as convinced that to say "I am" would not be correct because I was not there at that moment. Much later I was to learn of the vagaries of the subjunctive and optative moods of the verb.

On a more mundane and materialistic level I recall the day I decided that I would spend my life in the United States of America. In 1942 the American GIs had arrived in Ireland for training prior to the invasion of the continent. I had the opportunity to become friends with one of these soldiers. I also had the joy of tracking him down and visiting him again some twenty-five years later in his home in North Carolina and he and I remain close friends. On the day in question he gave me some packets of Wrigley's chewing gum, the like of which I had never seen before. I remember saying to myself something like, "I am going to go to where they can make chewing gum like this!"

In 1958 after completing high school and medical college I did just that and I consider this decision to be one of the best and smartest I ever made. I still am overwhelmed at the goodness of the people of the United States in their willingness to adopt me as a very poor immigrant with very few assets except curiosity and determination! Still my great surprise may be imagined when on my 50th birthday a large box of Wrigley's chewing gum arrived for me unexpectedly, with a letter of congratulations signed by

Mr. Wrigley himself. Somehow he had heard the story of the motivating dynamic of chewing gum!

I was fortunate to be able to earn scholarships from the end of grade school to the completion of my medical training. At that time in Ireland only grade school was free and my parents could not have afforded even the costs of high school. I did quite well in medical school and earned, in the British tradition, two "Firsts", one in pathology and one in pharmacology, the former with a gold medal.

Through all my developmental years I continued to be fascinated with the problems of human life and, what I would eventually learn was, the question of human existence and being. Unfortunately, all of these queries and interests had to be explored in my own reading because the scientific curriculum left no time for formal philosophy. However, by the time I had completed high school I already had some six years of Latin and classical Greek behind me, which would later prove to be most helpful as I began to explore the New Testament in the original language and the writings of great philosophers. I continued to read and, unfortunately, to understand relatively little.

In my medical education and later in the practice of surgery I became fascinated with the influence of faith on the healing process. This led to correspondence with Dr. Karl Menninger of the world famous Menninger Clinic in Topeka, Kansas. This dialog further stimulated my interest and curiosity and eventually led to my appointment as a graduate student in psychiatry at the Menninger School of Psychiatry. In this way my intellectual and clinical appetites were further stimulated and my childhood determination to "go to America" was actualized. After years of study this eventually led to certification in adult and pediatric psychiatry, addiction medicine, forensic psychiatry and later in psychoanalysis.

Shortly after completing training in psychiatry I was given the opportunity to become the director of the psychiatric training program at Marquette University Medical School in Milwaukee, Wisconsin and I have continued to practice in Milwaukee ever since. Many years later, at age 60 to be exact, I became a freshman in Marquette University Law School and went on to become a lawyer and a proud member of the Wisconsin Bar. This led naturally to extensive work on a national level in forensic psychiatry. My contemplation of perennial questions and issues, however, remained unabated and unsatisfied. This had led me to theological seminary where I focused on the psychological aspects of religious experience and then even later to graduate school where I obtained a graduate degree in Biblical languages. In retrospect I now find it fascinating that, from my parents' perspective, the apogee of the academic enterprise was for one to become a doctor, a lawyer or a minister.

Now, at the far end of my career, although the road is far from over, I have the opportunity to express my lifelong explorations, curiosities, conclusions and the distilled wisdom of a plethora of great teachers, at whose feet I have had the blessed privilege to sit. God has been good and perhaps these distillations will be of help to another curious chewing-gum seeker!

2006 has arrived and the path continues! The end is not yet! I am still ambulating!

Since the 2005 publication of 'The First Book of Wit and Wisdom' the search for wisdom and a knowledge of God and His creation has continued unabated but not frenetically. My beautiful and patient wife Leila of almost fifty years and our daughter Lorraine and the best daughter any man could ever hope for – the latter a specialist in internal medicine – continue to harass me frequently for "working so hard and so much." I have discovered, however, that it is very difficult to make others understand that sometimes and at certain stages of life, what was once work has become fun and a hobby.

No one can appreciate the tremendous joy I experience when I see children from the inner city of Milwaukee respond to loving treatment and to carefully chosen medication. It is all the more exciting to me to realize that most of these children are 'Title IX-teen Patients' which means that many practitioners in today's economically driven milieu have little or no interest in treating the disadvantaged.

My overseas activities have continued and this last year I have been involved in attempting to develop satellite schools in Ireland, the Far East and continental Europe for Oxford Graduate School. I hope to do the same in Jerusalem when the political situation is opportune. I have also had the pleasure of spending time in Romania helping resolve some legal issues relating to a number of missionaries. To explore some of the cities connected with the stories of Dracula was great fun!

Perhaps my most exciting and rewarding presentation this last year was to members of the American College of Forensic Psychiatry. I discussed my ideas on the presence of a religious sentiment in the acts of sacerdotal pedophilia, about which in recent years we have heard so much. The close intertwining of the sexual and religious drives remains a perennial fascination for me.

The greatest excitement of this last year was the arrival of my seventy seven year old brother Frank – the last of the clan – together with his beautiful wife Eleanor, who came to visit me in the United States, the land of my adoption. He was the first and only member of my family ever to visit me on this side of the Atlantic – in strict obedience to my mother's wishes and command! However, in contrast to the Biblical Able, she being dead could no longer speak and so he was liberated to visit his baby brother. This was one of the most gratifying experiences of my life as I proudly showed him the beautiful state of Wisconsin – from the Illinois line to the Apostle Islands. God has certainly given me an amazing and undeserved privilege to be able to live in such a beautiful land.

My studies in philosophy at the University of California have continued to be exciting and rewarding. This in large measure has been due to Professor William Hagan, who is as full of erudition as he is of gentle compassion, and whose relatives originally came from Dungannon, not far from where I was born.

I have continued to serve as the Editor in Chief of the Oxford Scholars Press and presently I am engaged in preparing a publication of some fascinating papers of members of the Oxford Society of Scholars.

The horizon from 'The Rear View Mirror' may be narrowing and in spite of some medical challenges this year it remains as exciting as ever.

Utinam logica falsa meam
philosophiam
total non suffodiant!


May faulty logic not undermine my entire
philosophy!

Many sermons today make as little demand on the intelligence of the listener as they did on their authors.

The most powerful generator may be paralyzed and rendered ineffective by a loose connection.

I was once an idealist until, having discovered that orchids smell better than vegetables, I tried to make orchid soup.

I may not have the ability to change events that impact me, but I can change how I respond.

Never say, "I am depressed." Rather separate yourself from the negative emotion and see it as a transient negative state. You are not your depression.

What the Promise Keepers need to keep in mind: Since the only real man is Jesus, it is only by a faith-based relationship with Him that men can ever become promise keepers.

All men have a consciousness of God in the
basement of their hearts, even if they do not
recognize its presence or reject it.

With the superstructure of our minds, the truth
of God is grasped by revelation.

All knowledge acquired by man, in the final
analysis, is the disclosure of God by God.

The fallacy of pantheism is that God can never
be equated with creation *per se.*

For those who have been confronted with the
reality of God no argument is needed and such
indeed is superfluous.

God's replies always surpass my requests.

My inability is overwhelmed by His ability.

The most powerful revelation from God is when your own name is called.

Whatever does an atheist do on Thanksgiving Day? Perhaps feel grateful that he was not born a turkey!

My God has never needed a hearing aid.

Salvation has always depended on feelings…
His!!!!

We are not saved by Grace; that is the heresy of
Sandemanism. We are saved by Christ through
the medium of Grace.

If my child as a member of my family is simply
'sanctified' through me, just think of what my
pup has!!!!

Men marry hoping that their wives
will never change.
Women marry hoping that their husbands
will change.
Both are to be disappointed.

A pleasing accent must never be confused with a
powerful anointing.

Pastors and counselors who break the personal confidences of the confessional are pariahs who blemish their professional oath.

If you cannot praise God for what you have, nothing will ever be enough.

Could it be that my zeal for Christ is sometimes motivated by pride?

When we confine ourselves to the areas in which we are knowledgeable, then we will never appear stupid.

It used to be that 'Christian' books were published to make knowledge public, but today the Church has a plethora of books of the pecuniary stamp.

The passion of pride is the handmaiden of narcissism.

Pride is the phenomenological representation of
low self-esteem.

Christians should not seek self-esteem, only
Christ-esteem.

Faith is an embryo implanted by the Holy Spirit.
You must take care to see that it continues to
grow and beware lest it be aborted.

When God microscopes me through the lens of Jesus, I am seen as clean as Christ is. This is the essence of Justification.

Pride is the only disease, which makes everyone but the patient sick.

I saw Jesus today, first in the timid eye of a little "coke baby" girl, then in the profound depth of love oozing from the eyes of a foster mother.

Before Naaman could ever be healed,
he had to divest himself, first of his pride,
and only then of his uniform.

The only possible way to grow up in Christ is to
grow down in humility.

I am most critical of Christians who
are most critical.

Don't steal; the government doesn't like
the competition.

Nothing has ever taken my God by surprise.

God knows that I ain't what I want to be,
and I ain't what I ought to be,
but I ain't what I'm gonna be,
and oh, thank you Lord,
I ain't what I used to be.

Practice does not make perfect,
it makes permanent.


The current emphasis on the mega-church is
most likely a monument to the flesh.


The Church appears to have fallen into the trap
of "Programitis" – more interested in building
programs than building people.

Good can only be appreciated against the
backdrop of evil.

There has never been the slightest danger that
God would be defeated in anything.

When confronted with any phenomenon that
claims to be religious or spiritual in nature, ask
whether the same could have been produced in
the total absence of Holy Spirit.

Much of what is practiced in the evangelical church today is the mere pseudo-sanctification of the secular.

I must remind myself constantly that only HE can see the big picture—the end from the beginning.

Geography will never be the answer to unhappiness between the ears.

Always try never to hurt anyone and accept the
fact that someone will always be hurt.

The Puritans strove to be pure from a Puritan
perspective and perhaps failed to see that the
only real issue is HIS PURITY.

Advice to young Christians: When the
Devil reminds you of your past,
remind him of his future.

My God does not exist in the
Past or Future tense.

The best preparation for living in the world
today is to focus on the world tomorrow.

The greatest mistake is to believe that you can
teach a child values while you yourself march to
a different drummer.

Many politicians consistently confuse change
and progress.

At times our nation has lost the will to do
something simply because it is right rather than
because it is expedient.

I find it amazing that many evangelicals write
expensive books about life before they have lived.

A cult is a congregation of isolated screwballs
pretending to be socially integrated.

The world's political systems have become a
mere incubator for personal aggrandizement,
patronage, pillaging and pecuniary
embellishment – often with the help of my taxes.

Open confession and sharing will detoxify the
most malignant and closely guarded secret.

Acute astonishment causes time to
pass more rapidly.

Many Christian leaders today appear to be more
interested in being cozy with the President than
in being crucified with Christ.

Power is always encased in an armored sleeve, in
which there is always a variety of hairline cracks.

Bad lawyers consider themselves to be a
privileged elite that slither between the worlds of
commerce, law and politics without much effort.


Bad lawyers; especially those in politics,
are those who oil the wheels of patronage
and corruption.


Most of the little wisdom I possess today came
through the pangs of hindsight.

Discreet private and very expensive health
care systems are used by politicians and rich
businessmen, who praise the cost-cutting
achievements of HMOs and the dedication
and professionalism of their staffs – but who
wouldn't be caught dead using one.

When a woman loses her man she starts
all over again; when a man loses his woman
he is already dead.

I have never succeeded by chance, only by choice.

To be exalted on the cross is to be placed on the
pinnacle of all my human potentialities.

One of the most important questions I have
ever asked myself: "Am I playing a game or am I
being played by a game?"

Sometimes God has used me when He couldn't
find anyone worse!

*Tout comprendre est tout pardoner.*

Often one has to complete an activity before
understanding fully the reason for the activity.

Being impressed with my own ignorance I have
struggled assiduously to dilute it.

Only stupidity ever threatens the composure
of God.

Christians should be more aware of
spiritual telegony.

An optimist is an individual who says that
this world is the best possible place to be; a
pessimist believes it.

The Irish and the English have long struggled to destroy what they have that is uncommon rather than working to expand what they have in common.

A basic strategic question: Is the goal worth the risk?

Is it not bizarre that millions of Americans this year will pay $25 for a book on dieting while half the world agonizes in hunger?

Many preachers appear to confuse inspiration with the botched stab of a lugubrious and well-fed forefinger.

The ideal psychiatrist or psychotherapist should aim to emulate the confidentiality of a deaf Trappist.

While definition of terms is basic to all communication and argumentation, there are some concepts, such as, for example, consciousness and time, which are so basic and primitive that no definition is necessary or indeed possible.

Many years ago while trying to sleep under
a tree in a tropical humid jungle I decided that
the devil had the aroma of the fecaloid rot of
a rain forest.

The evidence of genius is the ability to see
the obvious.

In the church of today, loyalty and
gratitude are such a rare commodity that
they deserve suspicion.

Time is a one-way proposition.

Memory is the ultimate seductress.

Impatience is the mother of all human errors.

For many people reality is a
disturbing inconvenience.

The single and most important function of
diplomacy is to postpone the inevitable.

When I hear the daily news and see what is
happening to our great nation I react with
outrage-fueled dedication to working for the
good of my country.

One of the effects of patriotism is to
dull the senses.


I am curious why congregations are referred
to as "flocks," because technically the term
"herd" refers to the domesticated and "flock"
to the undomesticated.


Politicians spend much time in fabricating a
buffer of plausible deniability.

The search for truth is to be guided more by logic than inspiration.

It takes only one liar to make an alibi.

I have struggled long to understand the full dimensions of my ignorance.

Perhaps the world's greatest oxymoron:
"Fighting for Peace."

Lying on your back has the effect of changing the
quality of your voice and will make you sound
unwell – a fact discovered by many employees
who call in sick.

It has been clearly demonstrated that there are
no bounds to the evil acts of men.

When I cannot control my own time, it means
that someone else is!

When conducting an interview, try to seat the
individual to be interviewed on your right. This
means that the individual will look at you from
the left and will engage the side of the brain that
is less critical and judgmental.

I cannot live in a vacuum and if I do not attempt
to look out for the welfare of others no one
will be there when I need someone to be on the
lookout for me.

Awareness of my own ignorance tends to make
me more accommodating.

Faith and Failure are similar, in that Faith
concentrates on certainty, while Failure obsesses
on the possible.

Lesson for American Liberals: Appeasement will
never eradicate the inevitable – only postpone it.

Sometimes God may permit me to fall, because that is what it may take to demonstrate to me that without Him I am nothing.

The real danger in failing is that we react with permanent paralysis.

Preachers should refrain from aiming at a degree of originality to which they are not equal or of which the subject under consideration will not admit.

Most corruptions of Christianity have arisen
from the indolence of its teachers.

Little success is seen in the preaching of the
gospel because little success is expected.

Seeking an explanation for behavior must not be
construed as making an excuse for behavior.

When a congregation grows to the point that the
pastor does not recognize the sheep, he is rich
but no longer a pastor.

When we are presented with an argument, we
should examine it carefully for flaws and defects,
and never let ourselves be dazzled by the rhetoric
or the prestige of an opponent.

The best preacher is the man with the
most grace.

The man who intensely desires knowledge will
not tolerate idleness.

Seminary education today seeks to teach how to
preach from the understanding when the only
preaching worthwhile is from the heart.

The worst criticism you can make of a sermon is
that it was witty.

In the pulpit outstanding eloquence,
erudite satire and personal charisma will
always be inadequate without the catalyst of
preparatory prayer.

Never try to preach humility, practice it.

Sermons that tickle the imagination usually miss
the conscience.

It is relatively easy for a preacher to expound on the spiritual value of poverty, when he is bringing in big bucks from variegated sources.

Pastors must leave the world to the people of the world.

To evaluate a man examine his library.

Sometimes more wit is used to cover
less wisdom.

Thucydides' practical view of democracy: "The
standard of justice depends on the power to
compel and in fact the strong do what they have
the power to do and the weak accept what they
have to accept."

No man's respect for old age extends to old eggs.
We all have our limits.

Good manners and soft words have brought
many difficult things to pass.

Three things will never come back to me: a spent
arrow; a spoken word; a lost opportunity.

Oh, the arrogance of a man who, when he finds
a woman for whom he believes nothing is too
good, asks her to take him.

Do all the good you can,
by all the means you can,
in all the ways you can,
at all the times you can,
to all the people you can,
as long as ever you can.

All eyes see God's benefits, but few see God.

Men's promises: Write them on the sands of
time, but not on a woman's heart.

A woman's advice is of small account, but a man
who does not take it, is of no account.

One smile for the living is worth twenty sighs
for the dead.

A swollen head is a curious disease – the
curious thing about it is that it is never caused
by the brain.

To live without God is to trust in a spider's web.

Never meet trouble halfway; let it do all
the walking.

It's no use galloping, if you are going the
wrong way.

When God puts a burden upon you, He always
puts His strong arm underneath.

Happiness is less doing what one likes, than
liking what one does.

Take time by the forelock.

A friend is one who knows all your faults and yet
loves you just the same.


It's very easy to be good, but it's very lonesome.


*Ad astra per ardua.*

Some men are wise, but most are otherwise.

Whether life is worth living or not depends
on the liver.

It is easy to see the silver lining in other
people's clouds.

You should always be ready to learn a lesson even
from a foe.

It is dangerous to be more interested in legality
than in morality.

He who refuses to forgive another breaks
the bridge over which he himself must
eventually cross.

They are never alone who are accompanied by
noble thoughts.

Happiness is not perfected until it is shared.

Never do what is wrong to demonstrate your
own rightness.

Sex used to have to do with love and life; now it is more concerned with narcissistic gratification.

To believe that something is true simply because I wish it so is superlative folly.

We become what we listen to, watch and read.

The worst bridges we cross in life are those we never come to.

Forensic science is based on the principle of criminal transference: the perpetrator will always take away traces of the scene and victim with him and will always leave traces of himself at the scene or on the victim.

In today's climate of political correctness there is no such thing as a small bald man, only one who is vertically challenged of scalp.

The secret to becoming a legend is to
always make your job look a lot harder than it
actually is.

Political language is the language of
manipulation, compromise and half-truths.

When Paul uses the formula, "It is written," he
is reflecting the Hellenistic formula that was
used when reference was made to the terms of an
unalterable binding legal agreement.

God calls me to be Christological in my thinking
so that I can be *Christophoros*, which means to be
a Christ-Bearer in society. This is the aim, sum
and substance of contextualization.

Socrates was convinced that there is such a thing
as an absolute standard of truth and justice,
right and wrong and that it is our duty to try and
discover it. How the mighty have fallen!

Sometimes as I observe the Evangelical Church
today, I am impressed at how few understand
Paul and how even they misunderstand him.

The essence of the absorption in the God type of mysticism was first whispered in the words of temptation, *"Eritis sicut Deus,"* – "Ye shall be as God."

Learn all you can so that you will be able to learn more!

Christian sanctification is when God takes the world out of me and I take myself out of the world.

Most evangelical preachers of today have not learned that good sermons are not the result of inspiration but of perspiration.

As a Christian I have struggled constantly to be like God while retaining as much of the devil as possible.

The essence of the Christian life is not knowledge and understanding but Obedience.

One of the reasons I admire Paul so much is that in spite of his greatness, he is capable of the deepest feeling. He, for example, can feel like a mother, can write as a father and can even call the mother of one of his friends, in a good humored way, his own mother. Both emotion and love flow from him.

God forbid that I should ever behave like a Gnostic-Christian who boasts of supposed enlightenment while acting as a stumbling block to an ascetically timid brother.

Without the aid of the Holy Spirit even the Scriptures may become a stumbling block.

A child will never develop adequate
internal controls if the parents say one thing
and do another.

Beware of any Christian leader who hobnobs
with political gadflys.

All new developments in the Church should be
taken, "*Cum grano salis.*"

A sexual revolution is the most effective and
insidious way to undermine the total morality
of a society.

The understanding of the Holy Spirit is
inextricably woven with the study of the
human spirit.

The Evangelical Church of today needs more
of Paul. We need to emulate six unknown
believers, namely, Speratus, Nartzalus, Cittinus,
Donata, Secunda, and Vestia, the martyrs
of Scilli, who, on the 17th of July, 180, were
obliged to state in evidence before the procounsel
what was in their box. Their reply revealed the
treasure of their souls when they replied, "The
books used by us, and besides these, the letters
of the holy man, Paul."

The foundation of Biblical anthropology is an
understanding of the relationship between Holy
Spirit, holy spirit, and human spirit.

I generally find it much easier to trust God when
I don't feel I need him.

I need to be humble and to appreciate the
fact that in every man there is the potential to
be my teacher.

I have long been impressed with the fact that those who are most gifted at raising money are often intellectually inferior and tainted with psychopathy.

Wisdom is most often the product of careful comparison.

If you have already begun the process of repentance, you are already a changed person.

It is sad but true that winners usually take the
opportunity to revise history.


Never make the mistake of constantly
anticipating that you will make a mistake.


As a rational being I inhabit a landscape of
metaphysical solitude.

Children do not learn either algebra or values
because they like algebra or values; they
assimilate the material because they want to be
like their teacher.

The practice of true morality is impossible
without *"noli nocere"* – "never hurt another."

All our desires, wants, ambitions and wishes
are based on the way we think. As our inner
thinking matures so will our desires.

My God has never needed a hearing aid.

The original "double dipping" is the preacher's sermons which become books, and guess who keeps the money.

Instead of praying for God's will, pray that He will give you the power and ability to do your part in actualizing His will.

My desire has been, not to make value
judgments, but merely to understand.

Grandiosity is often the external manifestation
of internal and unresolved sexual conflicts.

Many anti-abortion enthusiasts are not
simply pro-life, but are rather anti-personal
rejection, on the basis of identification with the
unwanted fetus. Thus, while they are ardently
pro-life, they are at the same time vehemently
pro-death penalty.

Why should we not expect your child to search
for filth on the Internet when it is practiced and
boasted of, without any sense of shame whatever
in Washington, and when it fills the national
news with sordid and explicit details.

Even presidents, kings, and emperors are
susceptible to domestic discord.

I always have to keep in mind that when
someone hurts me they only make me stronger.

Many people are more concerned with the appearance of propriety than with propriety itself.

The essentials of interpersonal skills:
+ Respect superiors.
+ Respect subordinates.
+ Respect is to be earned not demanded.
+ Never ask your subordinates to do anything you are not prepared to do yourself.
+ Always be on the lookout for the opportunity to give praise.

Compared to shame, death is nothing.

A rape victim is statistically more likely to be raped again than one who has never been raped.

Even as a child I was dissatisfied with seeking to penetrate the veil of phenomena as I sought to grasp the reality of things.

If your opinion is not changeable by fact, then it is already unreasonable and corrupt.

Complete doctrinal agreement will tend to
stagnate spiritual growth.

The essence of intellectual integrity is the
willingness to question answers.

True love is to continue to feel the same when
you do not get what you want.

My complete inability gives God an opportunity.

If I am unwilling to love the 'unlovable' then I am
unqualified to love the 'lovable.'

Poverty destroys personal dignity.

The Bible teaches that we should study to be quiet, not critical.

I become a busybody and meddler in the affairs of others when I refuse to look at myself.

Many evangelicals seem to believe that God's love is reserved for the 'lovely.'

Because of my background and training,
I find myself in an unbelievable position:
My evangelical friends think I am a heretic and
my psychiatric friends think I am nuts.
I know I am both.

Unity does not demand uniformity and diversity
does not demand divisiveness.

We live in a polluted society and few realize
that even the most modern pollutants had their
origin in ancient Babylon.

God changes attacks into advantages.

God says that I have been emancipated from the tyranny of sin by means of having been put to death to sin and having been enslaved to God in resurrection.

Even as the one act of Adam in life affected all of mankind, so the one act of Christ in death will affect all mankind.

The act of Adam had various aspects:

+ As a sin it produced disharmony in the universe.
+ As a transgression it precipitated the curse of a righteous Subjector.
+ As an offense it hurt the heart of God and produced estrangement between Him and His creature.
+ As disobedience it involved deliberate revolt against a loving and righteous authority.

The twelve apostles proclaimed Christ as the Son of David, whereas Paul heralded Him as the Son of God.

Captivity in and of itself will never dissipate the identity.

Men are not the natural enemies of religion;
they will support it if it is the religion of the
'God of the eon.'

I cannot understand why God forsook Him and
left His enemies unharmed.

Christ is the man who can. He is the power
of God and is God's executive who has been
spiritually endued for that purpose.

As the 'express image of God' the Son of God reveals Him.


What God does, we learn through His Christ. What God is, we learn through His Son.


Many evangelicals believe that faith is the confidence that God will do what we desire. This is faith in ourselves and is the basis for the current heresy of self-esteem.

Justification is only part of what I received. Did you ever see a judge acquit an accused law-breaker and then invite him to become his close friend?

"Falling from grace" is the result, not of breaking the law, but of the attempt to keep it—as a means of earning salvation.

The law must be practiced and administered, not within the parameters of obsessive-compulsive rigidity, but within those of common sense.

One of the most exciting and encouraging things God introduced into this world is death, for even as we confront it, we see that it is already beaten.

Human beings without values are mere animals… and that is an insult to my dog.

Faith uses obstacles as stepping-stones to God.

Anything that is worth doing always runs the risk of producing a mess.

When something that claims to have a spiritual basis is very big, then a prudent man will have doubts.

When I am selfish I am sinning and when I am sinning I am selfish.

A louse knows nothing about loyalty.


Use of the word "spiritual" is often a denial or
ignorance of the "natural."


Ecumenicity must be based first on the
commonality of the Word.

Being "in Christ" does not imply that we have
become automata or have lost our unique
individuality. It means, rather, that the
very essence and ultimate meaning of our
individuality have become transformed into the
similitude of the character of Jesus.

It is almost impossible to talk and to think
at the same time.

Spiritual "feeling" experiences tend to be
the desire of those who refuse to do the hard
work of Bible study.

The principal reason that I am not an evolutionist is that I do not have enough faith.

The best route to health is not Blue Cross, but Old Rugged Cross.

A man's library will show what the man is.

As I have matured and aged I have more and more been conscious of all that I do not know.

There is no basis for moving from a purely psychological analysis of my experience (it matters not whether theistic or atheistic), without already possessing a metaphysical framework in which the experience may be examined.

Never put up an umbrella until the rain starts.

To repeat an unkind truth is just as malignantly
evil as to invent a lie.

Do not stain today's blue skies with
tomorrow's clouds.

Nothing will make us so charitable toward
the faults of others as by thoroughly knowing
our own.

Truth must be preferred to personal feelings.

It is my conviction, based on over forty years
of observation that if the body needs medications
to relieve pain, it will not become addicted
to them.

The tragedy of the world today is that I often see
orphans with living parents.

I have learned that modern evangelical churches do not want pastors – they want promoters.

I experienced great comfort when it first dawned on me that nothing has ever dawned on God.

Evangelical seminaries have fallen into the trap of training for Place, Prominence and Prestige.

Today Evangelical pseudo-christian counseling
spends valuable time helping people discover
'Who they are,' when they should be
emphasizing 'Whose they are.'

My relationship to Jesus Christ continues to:
+ Excite me.
+ Upholds me.
+ Convicts me.
+ Strengthens me.
+ Weakens me.
+ Prods me.
+ Nurtures me.
+ Terrifies me.
+ Gladdens me.
+ Encourages me.
+ Bothers me.
+ Vivifies me.
+ Shames me.

It is not the woman's role to foster her husband's childishness – but I enjoy it!

Much of the discussion about spirituality today is rather about sensuality – feelings are confused with spiritual power.

Advice for teachers:

Maieutic: This is an adjective derived from the Greek word for 'mid-wife.' Hence it pertains to the art of assisting at childbirth and to the positive aspect of the Socratic method. Socrates pretended to be a mid-wife, like his mother, because he assisted at the birth of knowledge by eliciting correct concepts. He achieved this by his process of interrogation and examination.

In every man I meet there is something which
qualifies him to be my teacher.

Stay humble on the way up because you might
need it on the way down.

Every time I make a public address I try to obey
the Law of the "Four Bs:"
+ Be bright.
+ Be simple.
+ Be brief, and
+ Be gone.

There is only one thing worse than 'Majority Rule' and that is 'Minority Rule.'

The pathological basis of Irish politics: "You must never be the friend of the enemy of your great grandfather."

A rule of thumb for modern evangelical sermons: "Keep the meat, if there is any, and spit out the bones."

My interaction with God has often been very bad. First, I doubt Him; then I dictate to Him and then I debate Him. Eventually this leads to "I trust Him."

Hospitalization for addictive disease serves only two purposes. One, detoxification, and two, dissipation of pride, so that the individual may become free to become involved in the process of reconstruction and change.

Discouragement never comes from God.

God and I frequently have a disagreement. I pray
for what I want and He sends me what I need.

It is always a mistake to be more
concerned about your calling than you are
about your character.

It took me many years to learn to do the right
thing and to do it right.

There are at least five things that I can never completely know:

+ The origin of the universe or even of me.
+ The nature of a transcendent God.
+ The purpose of being and life.
+ The future that is reserved in God's hands.
+ The power of God that has the demonstrable ability to radically change a life.

In psychotherapy, the therapist works from the outside in and the patient works from the inside out.

Everyone I will meet today is looking for some change in themselves or in their life. My responsibility is to consider how I might be able to assist them in this endeavor.

The essence of "the good" is always the complete subjection of the will to God.

A hard lesson for me to learn was that "Decision Determines Destiny."

One of the most important reasons that I should love my enemies is because I made them.

A lesson many Christians need to learn: Use things, not people.

Age is more a psychological than a chronological issue.

I am happy and relieved to know that while my past has a vote it does not have a veto.

To make the claim that the world is
without meaning is to claim that science
will never be able to interpret it or derive
scientific laws to explain it.


The primary elements of the image of God
appear to be:
+ Rationality;
+ Self-consciousness;
+ Conscience; and
+ Choice.


Be suspicious of the mega-church for it often
represents dilution of the truth.

All that is truth will be able to
tolerate discussion.


If I refuse to give a reason for the faith
that is in me, then that may be the reason
I have no faith within me.


Once I am sufficiently mature to be willing to
give a reason for my faith I will be willing to
listen reasonably.

He who spiritualizes what he does not
understand is clearly demonstrating that fact.

To trash a fellow believer behind his back
is an example of the grossest form of
immaturity and carnality.

The greatest danger in mudslinging is that some
of it will eventually contaminate the slinger.

Unlike many of my alleged friends my God never resorts to mudslinging; instead He covers my sins with His love.

To refuse to permit discussion and disagreement is to mandate indolent acquiescence parading as tranquility.

Those who engage in debates in the name of Christ often appear more interested in the love of triumph than the love of truth.

Those who seek the new and novel in religion
and its practice are sure to be disappointed.


An abrasive defense is almost always the
sign of guilt.


Those who seek to cover up sin by being
oblivious to the obvious are as guilty as the
original perpetrator.

When therapists seek to evade personal mistakes by blaming the patient, they are demonstrating psychopathology that at least rivals that of the patient.

Some preachers consider truth to be the exclusive result of their personal exegesis.

It was very humbling for me to first learn that God can get along very well without me.

The racism of the Nazis eventuated in the
Holocaust; the sexual revolution of the 80s
eventuated in baby-killing for convenience
and without guilt.

He who does not actively forgive his brother has
actively participated in his sins.

As a general rule men seek loyalty first and only
then are they interested in commitment.

Be careful that you do not let your memories
destroy you.

Freedom is never free!

As you struggle toward an objective keep in
mind that second place is a first loser.

If you really want to make God laugh,
tell Him your plans!


Recent surgery convinced me that my lease
had run out and that now I am on a day to day
contract with God.


Entrepreneurs, because they need
constant stimulation and change, usually
fail in management.

It is usually prudent to expect the expected.

The worth of a man is demonstrated by the
principles for which he is willing to die.

The current anemia of the evangelical church is
directly related to the diminished interest in the
inspired Word in the hearts of our children.

Our society has lost the ability to
differentiate love and lust.

Often I have prayed to find myself in the right
rather than to learn what is right.

None are so credulous as those who faithfully
choose to believe in disbelief.

Many self-styled apologists for The Word
have apparently failed to recognize that the
Word needs no defense.

The worst thing about being retired is that
when I get tired from doing nothing I have
nothing to stop doing.

In my spiritual life business has almost always
been a synonym for barrenness.

I have usually tended to become preoccupied
with the impractical while forgetting that God is
thinking of the impossible.

God has promised to speak to me when I have
promised to listen.

A prayerful heart always puts God first.

It is easier to tolerate ignorance in another rather than conceit.

I need to be careful of all my words because words tend to have a life of their own.

I have never been finished when I lost – but I have been completely finished when I quit.

Falsehoods and lies grow best when the
light is excluded.

To be convinced that something is true simply
because we wish it, is undeniable folly.

Some Christian leaders today tend to follow
a course which they believe is right, being
totally unaware that what they are doing is
believing that particular course is right
because they follow it.

My experience is that I can be certain that in any
situation I will find two things:
+ The knowledge of what I ought to do.
+ An excuse for what I am inclined to do.

I have never yet wronged another but I have
ended up carrying the hurt.

The most effective therapy for injuries and hurts
afflicted by another is to forgive and then forget.

I have found that in my life the sweetest way to
take revenge is to make your enemy your friend.


Excessive argumentation dissolves and
does not establish truth.


I have discovered that when my tree of success
has grown tall, I have caught more wind.

I have been at my best and I have grown most
when another has pointed out my worst.

When a liar accuses me it is wise to
maintain silence.

I have always struggled to be slow
enough to be sure.

Reason, at times, is inadequate and
revelation is necessary.

Often I have confused my efforts
with God's power.

Every challenge and obstacle is merely an
opportunity in disguise.

It is a general principle of church life that the more material blessings you receive, the less spiritual you become.

Most of the bumps on the road of life can be softened by the practice of cheerfulness.

Wisdom is the result of carefully considering the whole picture.

I have discovered the best therapy for the evils others have done to me is not to remember them.

Even when my spiritual self has been at its best there have been some weeds as well as flowers.

Money is a medium which may be used as a universal Passport to everywhere – except Heaven, and a universal Provider of everything, except Happiness.

God never measures my success by what I have achieved, but by what He sees I have the potential to achieve.

My destiny will only be actualized when I intake my last breath.

The seeds of my defeats were planted in my victories.

The best way to assure one's history is to
live in the future.

Early I discovered that to kill time is to
murder opportunity.

All of God's promises are already actualized;
they merely are waiting for me to come along.

LOST – Yesterday.
Somewhere between sunrise and sunset;
The golden hours,
Each set with sixty diamond minutes;
No reward is offered,
For they are gone forever.

Many "fundamentalists" seem to be more
interested in winning an argument than in
winning a soul.

If you knew your exact clone would you
respect him?

Why do I not fear death? Because Jesus has "been there and done that."

Marriages are made in Heaven and often consummated in Hell.

Very often counseling is a promise without substance.

To focus on The Family rather than
to concentrate on The Christ may reflect
the current pseudo psychological seduction
of the church.

It is the grace of God that permits me to enjoy
today that which belongs to the future, such as
absolute righteousness.

What much of the church today needs is not
"Revival" but "Vival."

Early in my Christian life, I was convinced
that to be in the Word is great. It took me
many years to learn that to have the Word in
me is even greater.

I receive great confirmation when I pray, from
the knowledge that the word "Amen" is derived
from the Hebrew root which means, "He is
faithful." An excellent translation is "For Sure."

The outstanding characteristic of the Christian
character is gentleness.

I have had six years of personal psychoanalysis,
and I have experienced more radical change
through six hours of "Christian Music" therapy.

Is there healing in the atonement? This question
reveals serious ignorance as to the extent of our
salvation. The question is not whether, but when.

Long ago I discovered that it was much easier to
believe in God, than to believe God.

Questions to ask myself on reading the Word:
1. A Pardon to experience?
2. A Prohibition to obey?
3. A Practice to avoid?
4. A Person to emulate?
5. A Perfection to pursue?
6. A Passion to control?
7. A Peer to forgive?
8. A Prayer to pray?
9. A Proclamation to make?
10. A Provision to claim?
11. A Peace to enjoy?
12. A Promise to claim?
13. A Panic to avoid?
14. A Pain to ease?
15. A Possession to enjoy?
16. A Patience to practice?

Vice practiced in high places eventually becomes
fashionable, frequent and generally accepted.

Sometimes Evangelical theologians become so impressed with dogmatics that they tend to forget justification, reconciliation, redemption, forgiveness and adoption are all synonyms for "salvation in Christ."

In the days of Paul, the liberation or manumission of a slave could be affected by the solemn ritual purchase of a slave by a deity. The owner came to the temple with the slave, sold the slave to the god and then received purchase money out of the temple treasury. The difference is that the slave had, in all probability, previously paid the money into the temple treasury out of his own savings. In my case, Christ paid it personally and it did not cost me a penny.

One of the great challenges in my Christian life
has been the call to be persistent in my work and
consistent in my walk.

Perfect Love:
Slow to suspect. Quick to trust.
Slow to condemn. Quick to justify.
Slow to offend. Quick to defend.
Slow to reprimand. Quick to forbear.
Slow to belittle. Quick to appreciate.
Slow to demand. Quick to give.
Slow to hinder. Quick to help.

The greatest ability is dependability.

A hard lesson to learn: "Grow in Grace so that you will not Groan in DisGrace."

Many pastors appear to be determined to succeed in the struggle of moving from zero to hero, being oblivious to the fact that God has called them to a position of humility.

Berkely insisted that reality does not exist apart from the Knower, the Human Being, and that the existence of objects of reality depends upon the experience of the Knower.

The aim of mysticism is either *unio* or *communio*,
i.e., either oneness with God or fellowship
with God. It means either dissolution of the
human personality in God or sanctification of
the human personality through the presence
of God. Thus, mysticism either denies human
personality or affirms it.

It is well recognized in Greek grammar
that Paul uses the genitive case in two classical
ways, namely, the *subjective* genitive and the
*objective* genitive. In order to understand Paul
completely, these are insufficient because Paul
also uses a special type of genitive, namely,
the *genitive of fellowship* or the *mystical genitive*,
which indicates mystical fellowship with Christ,
thus, the phrase "of Jesus Christ" is often the
equivalent of "in Christ."

I have sinned but because I am "in Christ," I
am seen by God as perfect and as never having
sinned. I am justified.

How many Bible teachers today understand the
difference between arousal, vivification,
and resurrection?

There is always a danger in rousing the emotions
before securing the conviction of the intellect.

It is important to note that the Torah, as suggested by the etymology of the word, was not designed to describe historical situations, but to teach religious and moral lessons.

It is fascinating to note, what is an essential prerequisite to New Testament exegesis, that much of the New Testament writings are in many ways dissimilar from and show little influence of Paul and at times may actively differ from Paul's thought. This we find in Acts, James, Peter and the Johannine writings.

It is clear that Paul's view is that our eschatological salvation has already begun presently in Christ.

Paul's view of world history differed from the Greeks who believed in a repetitive cycle. He considered history as coming from God and moving toward the divine *telos* or consummation.

The letter to the Hebrews begins with a demonstration of the superiority of Christ over angels. This is quite understandable when we remember that the Mosaic Law was given to Israel through the agency of angels. It was long anticipated however, that there would come a time when angels would no longer be in control.

Forgiveness is interpersonal.

I have sinned and I have been forgiven.
It is not a question of merit or excuse.


If I demonstrate any wisdom today, it is because
I have already confessed the sins of yesterday.


The surest way to guarantee easier traveling
is to mend your ways.

Message to evangelical apologists: In an excess of
dispute, truth is generally lost.

The best way I can emulate Christ is to be as
unlike Jackson as it is possible to be.

When someone disagrees with me, it should
stimulate cognition rather than produce passion.

Many political administrations appear to know little about true leadership and merely free-wheel from crisis to crisis.

Too much hubris generally confronts its own nemesis.

Paul's theological thinking is not only central to the New Testament but it aggressively dominates the development of early Christian thinking.

I have been in parts of the world where I have seen men carry their god and I have tried so much to show them how my God carries me.

Wisdom is rather like gray hairs – they are generally not found in youth.

The Evangelical church has become an Arcadia – pretending to be lush and verdant, it is barren and bare; commanded to feed the sheep, its wares are often more suitable for goats. It has little to recommend it save its hedonistic admiration of Pan and like the Arcadia of old, Polybius could still accurately describe the Church as devoid of most things associated with pastoral care and bliss.

Few Americans appear to fully appreciate how
much God has blessed this nation.


The Evangelical church has been a 'shame
culture' rather than a 'guilt culture.'


The energy that drives the church today is
the craving for public approbation, self-esteem,
personal recognition, and exposure, rather than
the pricks of inner private morality
and *'suneidesis.'*

Heraclitus tells us that the words of Homer were a nurse for the mind of a child and that feeding the imagination on Homer's poesie should begin when we are scarcely out of our swaddling clothes. Such used to be the case in the Church and Christian homes regarding the Word.

The Christian Church appears to have forgotten that at the *Bema* there will be no stars without scars.

Thucydides, speaking of the Athenian character, reminds us of the spiritual and psychological value of hope – namely, that the hoping for something results in an 'as if' experience of having already possessed it. Thus should the Christian be molded and influenced by his hope.

Do not look for the faults as you pass through
life;
and even when you are forced to notice them,
it is wise and kind to be somewhat blind,
and look for the virtues behind them.


There is a dimension of the legal enterprise
that has frequently discomfited me, namely,
that competency and skill in argument remains
disparate from the merits of the case.


The path of the Christian pastor today is often
the razor edge between Scylla and Charybdis
– to be popular.

The response of Argus to the sound of the voice of Odysseus, after a lapse of so many years, should be a lesson to a world in which loyalty and commitment are the exception rather than the rule.

"To gossip" always ends up in the passive voice.

War, most often has good men on both sides dying for a worthless cause that has been reified by selfish politicians in "right" versus "wrong."

Aristotle did not believe that man is a
'political animal' but that man naturally is drawn
to living in a *'polis'* – an illustration of
the significance of *'koionia.'*

Punishment which is unending can only be
considered legally to be more than Retributive
and must be thought of as Vindictive.

A caricature looses all of its force if it does
not bear a recognizable resemblance to the object
it ridicules.

A hope of immortality was a relatively late
development in the religious experience of Israel.

For the Christian, from the Lord's viewpoint,
failure is never absolutely final and irrevocable.

The convicting power of the Holy Spirit on
sin acts like the heat of the sun on the wings
of Icarus.

God is not in the world seeking seekers – He is
seeking sinners.

Accept the wisdom of Sophocles and never
aspire to personal greatness because in such a
path lies destruction.

Often I prefer not to climb out of my
thoughts and my preference is to aspire to and
retire to the contemplative.

Mistaken Notions of Theology:

1. There is a Hell for those who are beyond Pardon.
2. There is a purgatory for those who are Pardonable.
3. There is a Paradise for those who have been Pardoned.
4. There is a limbo for those "souls" who remain Dormant.

The secret of happiness is to be thoroughly preoccupied with something.

To consider your epitaph is to put your life under scrutiny.

My plethora of mistakes in life have not been as important as what I have learned from them.

The evil of ecumenism is that the principle of sacrificing truth in the interests of unity is invidious.

The fabricated accusation of racism is one of the most malignant forms of racism because it leads to racism.

Life is exciting and valuable until it
becomes an inconvenience.

Man's technological expertise has
surpassed his moral competence.

Our advertisements reflect the color of
our national soul.

The beginning of wisdom is the definition
of its terms.

Love is an action word, and if not done, is not.

When Juvenal complained that the Ornontes
had long ago flooded into the Tiber, he was an
accurate prophet of the racism of today.

The prudence of today is an edifice built on the mistakes of yesterday.

God forgives and then forgets; many of his children "forgive" and save the material to be used as ammunition against you later.

In every interpersonal relationship there is an energy exchange. In the relationship with God the energy is the Holy Spirit. In both, the energy exchange is the *sine qua non* of relationships.

When I accept you as you are, I do you love.


We are not told to love our neighbors but to
behave lovingly toward them.


Love exists in concentric circles
while hate is punctiliar.

To be orthodox is often a defense
against self-exposure.

My citizenship may be in heaven but my feet
are planted on *terra firma*.

He, who ridicules the simple,
is simple in his ridicule.

All Psychology is as simple as A, B, C – the examination of Affect, Behavior and Cognition.

When you sin against God, He will forgive; but when you offend His Church, expect harsh consequences.

Worship is to:
1. Quicken the conscience by the holiness of God.
2. Feed the mind by the truth of God.
3. Purge the imagination by the beauty of God.
4. Open the heart to the love of God.
5. Devote the will to the purposes of God.

When I follow tradition, because I am afraid
there might be an error of my own judgment, I
have already compounded the evil.

The desire to become Christ-like involves a
willingness to change all the spurious tendencies
in my personality which opposed absolute and
total control by Christ.

Being "in Christ" is as the fetus is to the
mother – the fetus is in the mother and the
mother is in the fetus.

Worry is an attempted assault on the
integrity of God.

Show me the friends you hang around with and
I will show you the friends you will hang with.

On occasion I have been willing to sabotage the
future for the present.

Much of what passes for theological study in the Evangelical Church today can accurately be described as "Tabloid Theology."

So that I do not feel alone I constantly remind myself that Jesus approaches everyone with forgiveness on His mind.

The outstanding characteristic of the human personality is the need for forgiveness.

Romans Chapter One shows that:

Confusion about Deity leads to
Confusion about Humanity, which leads to
Confusion about Identity, which leads to
Confusion about Sexuality.

I have been willing to give God the credit – but
rarely the cash.

I always have had a tremendous urge to
learn the most I can learn of whatever there
is to be known.

Faith is not a mere cognitive or affective response
but a persistent attitude about what is real.

Professed evangelicals often confuse
Ritual with Religion.

I have long struggled to understand the
significance of Jesus Christ in my life.

For me the 'Inspiration of Scripture' means that its writers were touched in some mysterious way by transcendent realities.

Many problems in the understanding of Holy Scripture result from the failure of Bible students to appreciate fully that all human discourse is communicated in metaphor.

For me, the perennial excitement of the resurrection is that while Jesus has become invisible, He has paradoxically become more present and accessible.

One of the greatest miracles is how God turns Losers into Leaders.

My sins are not forgiven – I AM!

My contentment is based on the knowledge that God has given me just as much as He can trust me with.

Sometimes it is easier to withstand Adversity
than Prosperity.

In Christ I have an endless hope,
not a hopeless end.

Some use words to communicate Knowledge;
others use words to cover ignorance and call the
process Rhetoric.

Decision determines Destiny.

Believe not everything you hear;
By God's Word try all you read;
Only thus shalt thou not fear
And on His truth thou shalt feed.

Love, pleasure and happiness; all must be
shared to be enjoyed.

He who knows Jesus only as Savior has only
gone halfway, and needs to travel to the point
where he knows Him as Lord.


Patients never consult a physician for mere
medical care; they come looking for magic
and miracles.


The standard for Duty of Care for
physicians is that of the community and
not that of the HMO.

Much of modern evangelism has been designed
to appeal to the soul of the sinner rather than to
the vivification of his spirit.

Educators are confused when they teach that
children learn because they have a desire for
knowledge or mastery. Children learn because
they want to be like their teacher – models, on
the basis of identification.

In order to reach the highest I must be willing to
meet God at my lowest.

God demands the U-Turn of *Metanoia*.

Insistence of relevance is the first step
toward syncretism.

My future development will be determined
more by the promise of the future than by the
pain of the past.

Grace is not a license to sin.

Man is a contradiction for when the Law says,
"Thou shalt not," it awakens in him a desire
to do the very thing that God prohibits. And
it is a blessed fact that, when the sluice gates
of grace are opened wide, so that there is no
condemnation no matter what he does, he looses
the desire to sin, and finds, in the very grace
which guarantees immunity, a latent power
which enables him to rise above the very sin
from which he is now liberated.

Creation did not begin in chaos, but in Christ.
Creation will not end in ruin wrought by man,
but in reconciliation wrought by the blood
of Christ.


All of the New Testament, save the writings of
Paul, were limited in their scope to the terrestrial
as to space and to the eons as to time.


In the constant struggle against denial and
distortion, accuracy becomes the foundation
of truth.

As God's complement, Christ is the answer to philosophy: as our complement, He is the end of religion.

There is always a danger in mistaking enthusiasm and noise for the quiet yet powerful operations of the Spirit.

The *sine qua non* of greatness is service.

The church has moved from character to
personalities and from heroes to celebrities.

The family must remain the solid foundation of
a healthy society.

Often the best way to be effective for God is
to sit still.

When you wash someone's feet, be careful about
the temperature of the water.

An example is always more effective than
a lecture.

An unfair alternative to revelation is speculation.

Every time I have agreed with God to proceed
with the possible, He has undertaken to take
care of the impossible.

I have found that the best place to develop a
proper focus on life is in a cemetery.

My prayer for my only child, my daughter, is that
in her life she will focus on what I have learned,
and not on what I have accomplished or on the
mistakes I have made.

Many Christians delight in focusing on
reigning with Christ as an eschatologic event,
but refrain from seeing it as a mandate for
the present moment.

Biblical truth must not be taught as
commandments of men or the commandments
of men as Biblical truth.

When I make a statement of which I do not have
definitive conviction I am arranging for myself to
be less sincere when I speak next.

It is often difficult for superior men to be
loveable and compassionate, but Socrates
managed to do it.

How I would like to identify with Socrates!
A practical man and yet a mystic;
A sensualist and yet an ascetic;
A skeptic and yet convinced of human
capabilities.

It is alleged that the representation of the
Passion of Jesus is gross and emotionally
harmful, while the constant representation of
blood, gore, killing, murder, abortion and rape is
entertainment.

The essence of mysticism is the discovery of a way to God, directly through inner experience without the mediation of reasoning. The constitutive element is immediacy of contact with the Deity.

Without exception, "election" in Scripture is always for the purpose of blessing; yet those who place a disproportionate stress on "election" always seem to have condemnation in mind.

Every personality tends to gravitate to the company of its own kind.

Plato pulled no punches when he stated unequivocally that the very wealthy cannot be morally superior.

When you tend to make much ado about nothing, you will likely have little left to make ado about something when this is appropriate.

The true sense of each word is what it communicates to others.

So often in the past I have treated God's
commandments as if they were political
recommendations and something to be voted on.


I need to be more interested in the power
at work within me than the power I can generate
by myself.


I have discovered to my amazement that God's
generosity has always exceeded my specific need.

My first and best teacher in psychiatry, Dr. Karl
Menninger, taught me that "generous people
are rarely ever mentally ill, because giving is the
highest level of living."

Cryptic lack of integrity will eventually and
always become manifest.

When it comes to my personal sins and mistakes
in the past I have one basic rule: "Don't hide it,
but don't publish it."

The strategy of many Christians is never to let
you get past your past.

It is a sad fact that in the Church today, we
should not have high expectations regarding the
integrity and loyalty of fellow believers.

Once another individual succeeds in making me
angry, he has begun to control me.

The ultimate aim of all true religion is to change
the focus of attention from narcissism to God.

The hope of immortality must ever remain
subordinate to and dependent upon faith in
a loving God. Without this dimension the
question of immortality is not a religious issue
but remains essentially a narcissistic endeavor.

An act if done for the sake of resultant pleasure
or profit cannot be considered a moral act.

In Religion and in Ethics, the primary aim is to
remove Self from the focus of interest
and concern.

The Biblical doctrine of Immortality is
widely misunderstood in that its three special
characteristics are ignored:
1. It is a doctrine of Resurrection and not
   of immortality.
2. Resurrection is not an inherent human
   right but a gift from a loving God.
3. It is not a doctrine of rewards and
   punishments, but is a proclamation to
   the universe of the inherent joy of love
   and the inherent misery of selfishness.

The Stoics taught an Indifference to death
but the Christian Gospel demonstrates Victory
over it.

To say there is no such thing as tragedy in
human life is denial, but to demonstrate it
transformed from tragedy into glory is the power
of faith.

Only God is Immortal, but out of His love and
bounty, He is willing to bestow immortality on
those who do not possess it by nature.

It is a Hellenistic assumption that the "soul" in itself is inherently immortal.

It must be kept in mind that the word 'eon' (*aionos*) has primary reference to the quality of an age and not to its infinity.

My hope is not of a mere survival of death but of a resurrection that results in a whole new order of being, of which the chief characteristic is fellowship with God.

The essential ingredient of sin is separation from
God, from self, and from others.

The dynamic of justification is that God looks at
me through Jesus, as through a pair of glasses,
and suddenly I am seen as PERFECT.

As the result of coming alive in Christ my Guilt
has been removed, but that does not necessarily
remove my Shame.

My Perennial Problem: "I have so often
wanted to "put on" Christ without first
"putting off" self."

Difference is a mere challenge to thought and
not evidence of an antagonist.

An evidence of evangelical idiosyncrasy and
hypocrisy: Those who write the most about
psychotherapy have the least experience in
actual practice.

The tragedy of the Evangelical Church today is
that we desire the experiential ecstasy of power
without the hard work required in the search
for truth.

It took me a long time to learn that there cannot
be a filling until there is first an emptying.

Often I have desired the power without fulfilling
the conditions.

Power comes only after there is subjugation of
the self to Christ.



Self-denial is an old-fashioned word that is rarely
heard from evangelical pulpits.



Power is not a once in a lifetime occurrence that
lasts until the resurrection.

"Be filled with the Spirit!"
1. A present tense.
2. An imperative mood.
3. A plural number.
4. A middle voice.


There has been a gradual loss of a physician's ability to examine and diagnose without super-sophisticated instrumentation.


When a physician is placed under the economic and time constraints of the insurance and HMO-driven market, medicine then ceases to be a helping profession and degenerates into a hard-hearted market-oriented business.

Doctors are no longer primarily healers but have
become insurance servants.

Adolescents may choose their music –
1. As a tranquilizer – to obviate the need
   for thinking.
2. As an expression of rebellion
   against adulthood, parents and the
   "establishment."
3. On the basis of identification with an
   individual or group.

There is often a fatal attraction between certain
types of music and illicit drugs.

Being dishonest with others is less evil than
being dishonest with one's self.

The basis of society and of the nation is not the
school, but the home.

The values I practice today reflect the first five
years of my life.

A journalist who fabricates to franchise
is despicable.

He who believes that the press is responsible,
objective or ethical has already bought the
Brooklyn Bridge.

As Congress is controlled by lobbies, the Press is
controlled by advertisers.

An excessive preoccupation with "rights"
generally is associated with diminution of the
idea of "responsibilities."


Often I have been more preoccupied with
whether I "could" than with whether I "should."


My ambition has become distorted when my
aspirations have out-grown my capabilities.

No matter how low I have fallen, God has never
yet let go of my hand.


Forgive her/him even though she/he has so
vigorously tried to hurt you, because you both
will again need each other.


Sometimes I have striven to be so intellectual
that I no longer needed faith.

Intellectualism usually douses the power of God.


Denominations often appoint people whom
God cannot use.


When I stand before God it is always
without my disguise.

Pastors may be smart to their parishioners, but their smartness may make them ugly to God.

God's blessing on your life should never be confused with God's presence in your life.

You will never stumble if you are on your knees.

I am so impatient that I wait in a hurry.


There have been times during which I have
confused freedom from the law with freedom
from accountability.


God is so strange in His choices – He generally
chooses the most unlikely.

My sins were injected into Christ when He was
on the cross; His righteousness was injected into
me when I exercised faith.

Never confuse meekness with weakness.

The commonest reason that Christians are
reluctant to confess their failures is that they fear
humiliation at the hands of other Christians.

When you make a decision to shut your eyes to
the truth, even if it is to protect your friends,
then it matters not how good your eyes may be.


I often wonder whether I am pursuing a course
because I believe it is right or whether I believe it
is right because I am pursuing it.


Falsehood and mendacity are like a fungus,
because the less they are exposed to the light of
day the more they flourish.

I never need to pray for God's will to be revealed to me; I already know His will but I need to pray for His strength and desire to do it.

An example of consideration of the needs of another: Before he drank the poison Socrates said: "I prefer to have a bath before drinking the poison, rather than giving the women the trouble of washing me when I am dead."

When I focus excessively on "election" it may be coming out of my own pride and may in effect, be my "election" of myself.

When I follow tradition, because I am afraid
there might be an error of my own judgment, I
have already compounded the evil.

When we permit a child to be immersed in
violence, whether through the written word,
visual representation or by example, we will tend
to produce violence in the child.

A child will tend to end up with the same
values and internal controls that the parent
internally possesses, not those that the parent
pretends to have.

I am less concerned by a man's outward professions than I am by his inward convictions.

In criminal cases I see bad people at their very best and in divorce cases I see good people at their very worst.

The effects on children of being exposed to domestic violence is worse than being the victim of domestic violence.

Advocates for battered women are often more difficult to deal with than battered women.

Children need both parents or at least the best possible combination of both parents.

*"Amor enim compendiosissima ad Deum via est."*
Wisdom often takes the long way home, while "love is the shortest way to God."

Dia dhiabh agus beannacht
De oraibh go Leir!


May God go with you and may God's blessings
be on all of you!

ISBN 141209169-1

Edwards Brothers Malloy
Oxnard, CA  USA
August 12, 2013